Bella's New Digs

For Ariella, my Bella

Published in 2021 by Connor Court Publishing Pty Ltd

Copyright © Nick Dyrenfurth (text), © Andrew McIntosh (illustrations)
All Rights Reserved. Not to be reproduced without the permission of the Publisher.

Connor Court Publishing Pty Ltd
PO Box 7257
Redland Bay QLD 4165
sales@connorcourt.com
www.connorcourtpublishing.com.au

ISBN: 978-1-922449-61-0

Cover Design Andrew McIntosh

Printed in Australia

Bella's New Digs

Nick Dyrenfurth

Andrew McIntosh

Bella lives way up on the Moon.
Lives up, up, up there in a hot pink balloon.
Lives all alone, except for her cat ...
Bo and his mate, little Billy the rat!

The moon, Billy says, is made of Swiss cheese ...
the poor thing sulks inside, scared that she'll freeze.
But nothing scares Bo. Not pink garish balloons.
Not yawning moon craters. Not rocky space dunes!

'These are our digs,' sing Bella, Billy and Bo,
'No parents or teachers saying "No, no, no, no!"'

They all dine together and cuddle at night,
eating pizza and pasta and Turkish delight!

How did these three end up, up, up on the Moon?
They hurtled through outer space whistling a tune.
Strapped to a rocket-ship called the 'Rat Pack',
chock full of socks, doonas, lollies and snacks!

'These are our digs,' sing Bella, Billy and Bo,
'No parents or teachers saying "No, no, no, no!"'

But one day their pet cow runs away with a spoon,
leaving them sad and thirsty up, up on the Moon.

The very same night, naughty thieves steal the larder, leaving not a crumb, making three hungry lives harder!

The Moon, they decide, is a dangerous place.
'Crikey! It's time to find new digs in space!'
They speed off to Mars, red planet of plenty,
no thieves to be found; no bellies left empty.

'These are our digs,' sing Bella, Billy and Bo,
'No parents or teachers saying "No, no, no, no!"

Then one Martian day, Billy goes missing!
Bella is sobbing! Bo starts hissing!

The very same night, naughty thieves steal the larder, leaving not a crumb, making two hungry lives harder!

Mars, they decide, is a dangerous place.
'Crikey! It's time to find new digs in space!'
They speed off to Venus, white planet of plenty,
no thieves to be found; no bellies left empty.

'These are our digs,' sing Bella and Bo,
'No parents or teachers saying "No, no, no, no!"'

Then one Venus day, Bo went missing.
Bella's alone! No cuddles, no kissing.

The very same night, naughty thieves pinch the larder, leaving not a crumb, making one hungry life harder!

Venus, Bella decides, is a dangerous place.
'Crikey! It's time to find new digs in space!'
She flies off to Pluto, dark (dwarf) planet of plenty,
no thieves to be found; no belly left empty.

'These are my digs', sings Bella with a sigh and an oh.
'No parents or teachers saying "No, no, no, no!"'

Then one Pluto day, poor Bella goes missing.
Misses her friends, and their cuddles and kissing.

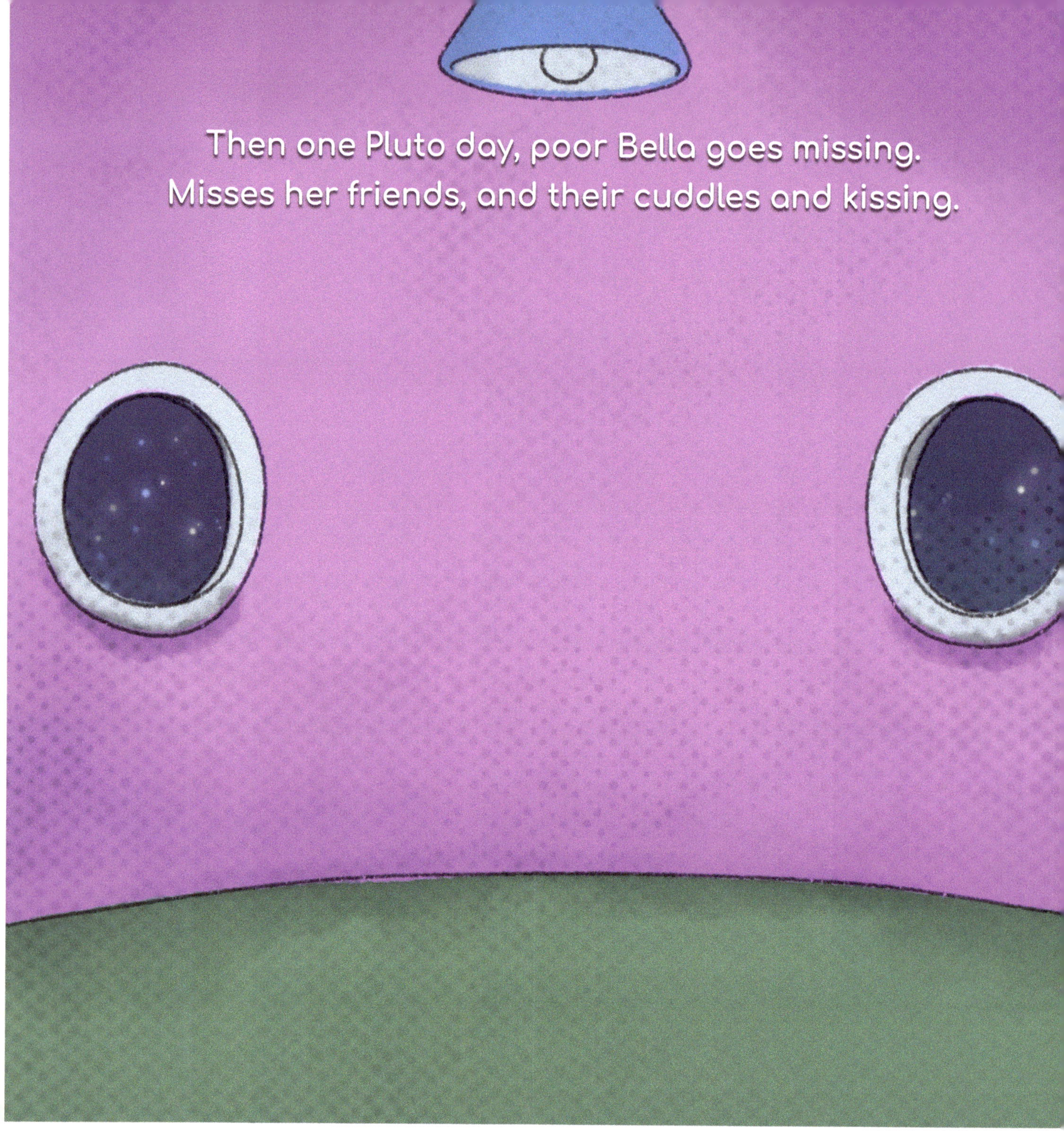

The very same night naughty thieves pinch the larder, leaving not a crumb; making hungry life harder!

Deep outer space is the loneliest place.
So Bella flies home to digs that are ace!
Back home to the Earth, blue planet of plenty,
no thieves to be found; no bellies left empty.

'These are our digs,' sings Bella as she goes,
'No parents or teachers saying "No, no, no, no!"'

Once upon a time, Bella lived up, up on the Moon,
until she tidied and packed away her hot pink balloon.

Bella ran rings around Saturn, Uranus, Mercury...
Jupiter, wow, what a great curiosity!
Goodbye to Venus, to Pluto and Mars!
Goodbye to a ceiling of three billion stars.

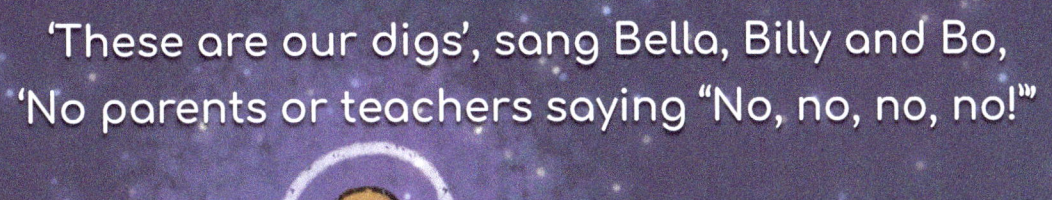

'These are our digs', sang Bella, Billy and Bo,
'No parents or teachers saying "No, no, no, no!"'

Very same night naughty thieves pinched the larder,
they left not a crumb – three bellies much larger!

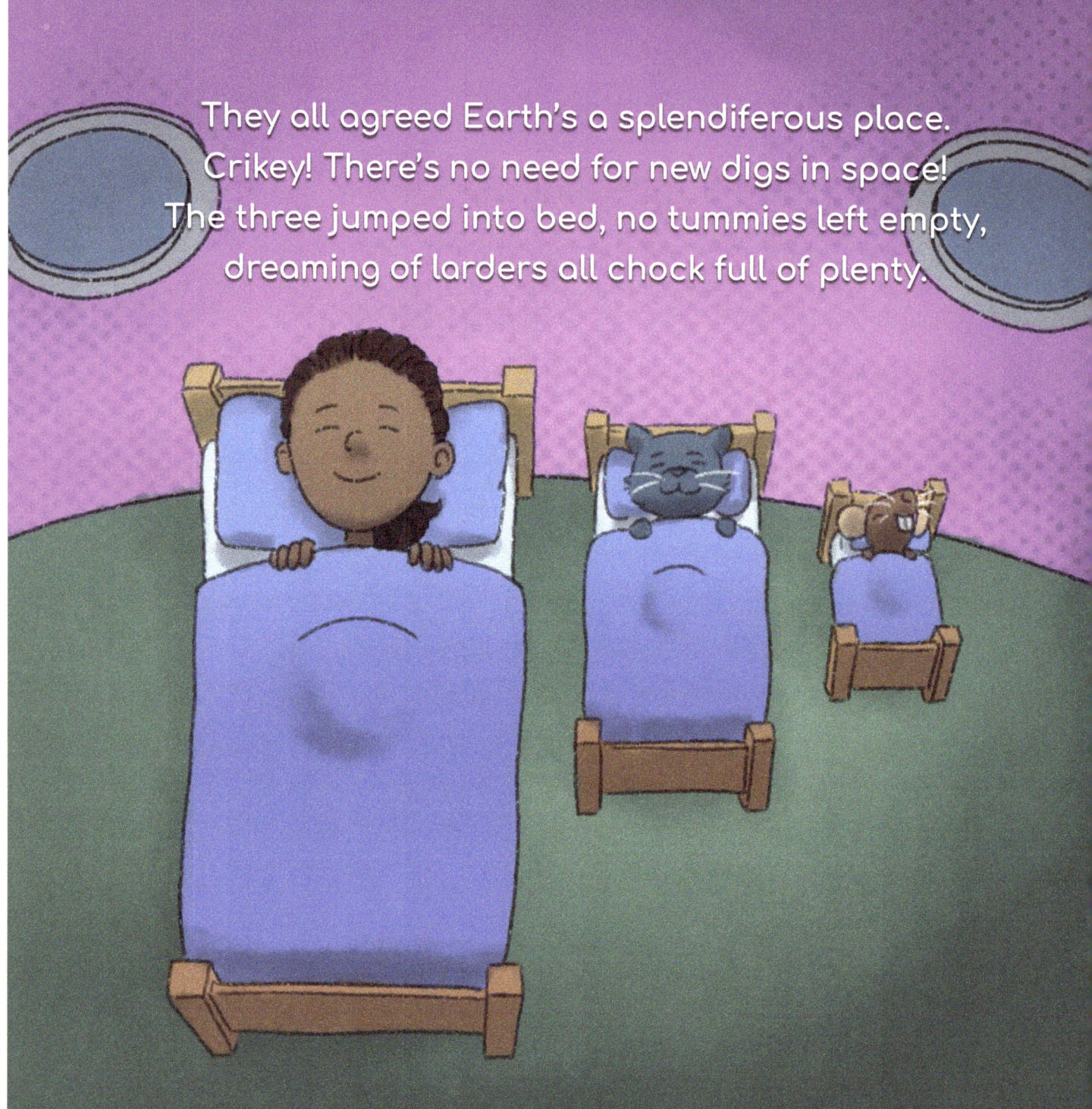

They all agreed Earth's a splendiferous place.
Crikey! There's no need for new digs in space!
The three jumped into bed, no tummies left empty,
dreaming of larders all chock full of plenty.

'These are our digs', sang Bella, Billy and Bo,
'With parents and teachers saying "Yes, yes and no!"

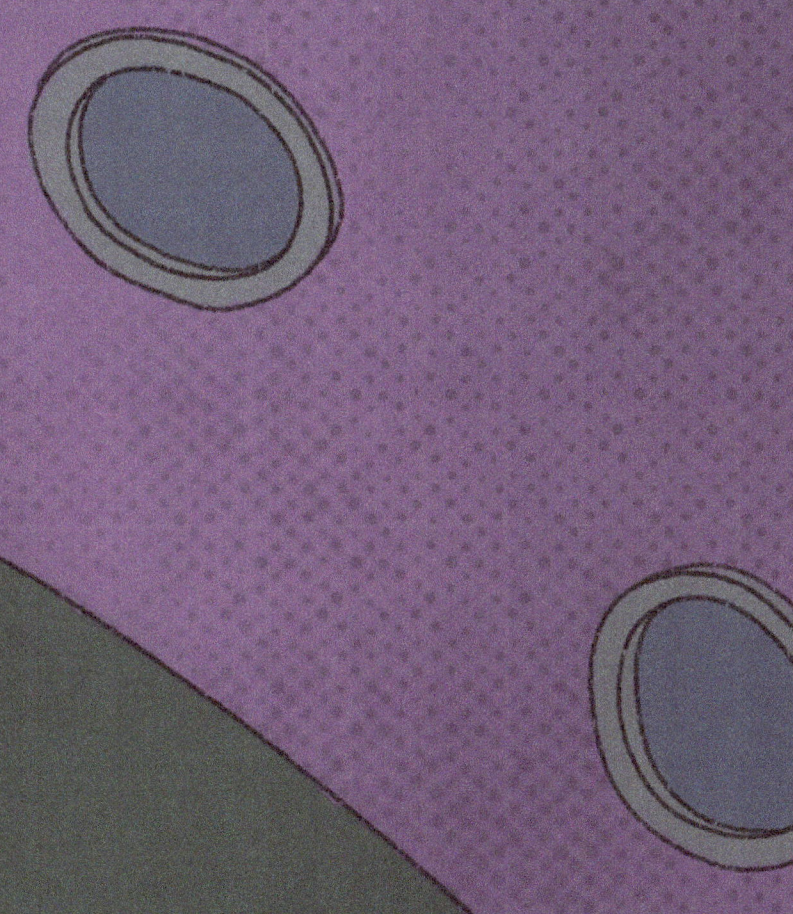

www.ingramcontent.com/pod-product-compliance
Lightning Source LLC
Chambersburg PA
CBHW051629170426
43195CB00044B/2981